T0199000

Can You Hear the Animals?

Book One:
The McPherson Family

Through animal communication, this collection of light-hearted children's compilations is aimed at creating awareness and instilling compassion, empathy, and respect for all life into young readers' minds and hearts.

Tracey Kehler

Illustrated by Kara LaRose

Balboa Press books may be ordered through booksellers or by contacting:

Balboa Press
A Division of Hay House
1663 Liberty Drive
Bloomington, IN 47403
www.balboapress.com
1 (877) 407-4847

Because of the dynamic nature of the Internet, any web addresses or links contained in this book may have changed since publication and may no longer be valid. The views expressed in this work are solely those of the author and do not necessarily reflect the views of the publisher, and the publisher hereby disclaims any responsibility for them.

Any people depicted in stock imagery provided by Thinkstock are models, and such images are being used for illustrative purposes only.
Certain stock imagery © Thinkstock.

ISBN: 978-1-5043-4800-3 (sc)
ISBN: 978-1-5043-4801-0 (e)

Library of Congress Control Number: 2015921116

Print information available on the last page.

Balboa Press rev. date: 12/30/2015

BALBOA
PRESS
A DIVISION OF HAY HOUSE

Dedication

The stories in this book are dedicated to all of the animals who are and ever have been true companions to us, your human caregivers. Your dedication and commitment to us as tried and true friends reveals unconditional love and companionship in a world that would otherwise be lacking in purpose, character, humor and emotional warmth.

I often wonder what our world would be like without the presence of animals to remind us of the simplicity of life and our own true nature of longing for peace, harmony, humor and love in the world.

Thank you animals, large and small, near and far, past and present, for being with us in all kinds of ways and for bringing us messages of love, laughter and some of life's most valuable lessons!

"Loveable Luke" whose spirit lives
on in Animal Kingdom Heaven

Acknowledgements

I would like to acknowledge and express my gratitude to my wonderful friend and "soul sister", Lindsay Lewis, for never giving up on me and always encouraging me to shine my own light. Without her loving support and undying listening ear, the path that I am walking today would surely not be happening. As an empath and psychic, Lindsay has spent countless hours inspiring me and so many others to discover their true divine purpose. Thank you for being such a wonderful friend, light and "soul sister" for me, Linds!

I would like to extend my gratefulness and appreciation to Victoria Sorensen. Vicki is a wonderful young spirited lady who has a true ability to put herself in a child's shoes. Vicki has created numerous play environments for her own grandchildren, clearly demonstrating her empathy and understanding of remembering what *fun* is for kids, often a forgotten language for many of us as we grow up! It's truly a gift to be able to relate to and create for children when we become adults. Vicki has this gift. Thank you, Vicki for allowing me to include Forest City, Sit Tea Haul, Bored Walk and Pirate Property in making this children's book just a little more fun! I have spent many moments meditating in Forest City myself. I thank you for providing such a creative space for my own imagination to flourish!

And to my niece and illustrator, Kara LaRose, I extend my most heartfelt warmth, gratitude and love as she has graciously extended her amazing art talents and time to this work! I am most fortunate and forever indebted to Kara's efforts and abilities and her eagerness to be a huge part of this project! Kara, without your input, talent and enthusiasm, this book in its entirety would not exist! Hats off to you for believing in it, but more so for believing in yourself! I can't thank you enough for sharing in this experience with me and I hope there will be many more opportunities for both of us to come!

Molly McPherson
And Her Big Family

"My name is Molly. I am a person.
I have a family. My last name is McPherson."
Molly McPherson has a brother and sister
and a mom and a dad they call Mrs. And Mr.

"My family is bigger than that though, you see
There's Suzy and Randy and Emma and me."
Then there's Alf and Ruby and Dixie and Dawn
and don't forget Philly who's always out gone.

Miley is shy and soon to be Mom
to one or two babies or more that may come.
Molly McPherson and her family
communicate daily 'bout what life should be.

Doctors and lawyers and teachers and such
Then Molly asks Suzy, "Do you need that much?"

When Molly McPherson is quiet and calm
her animals talk to her - tell her what's wrong.
Dawn has a sore tummy and Alf feels sick too,
And Randy thinks Emma has nothing to do.

Ruby is hungry and Suzy does worry
that Phil won't come home soon in any big hurry!
Dixie is happy and so too is Miley.
For both of these sisters are joyous and smiley.

"My name is Molly and as you can see
my family consists of so many and me!"

If you're ever alone and feeling so blue
then talk to your animals. They have feelings too!
Be kind and courageous, they might say to you
Just smile and suddenly you're no longer blue!

So talk to your family - the animals and you.
Don't forget them, they're listening. They want to talk too!

Phil
The Big Orange Cat

Phil, the big orange cat sat down one day.
I could see from his eyes that he wanted to play.
But he couldn't speak English, so I didn't understand
exactly what thoughts or what game he had planned.

As he slowly got up with his tail in the air
and he stretched and he yawned and he looked over there.
I could sense in a flash what he wanted to do.
It was surely as if he was tying his shoe!

As he purred and he chortled like cats often do
I could swear I heard something. I said, "I never knew!"
If I truly am listening, I can hear him speak loudly
He is speaking *my* language so boldly, so proudly!

If I am a person and Phil is a cat
We can speak the same language. Now imagine that!

Then I knew in a moment what he wanted to do
when he tied up his laces and exclaimed, "I love you!"
He was off to the forest to play Hide-n-Go-Seek
And he asked me to join him, help find him a creek.

"Why a creek?" I exclaimed, as he bounded away,
And he told me in English, "It's the best place to play."
As I followed believing that I understood
Phil's message, Phil's language - I would follow, I would.

We pranced through the forest taking turns being leader
I followed, he followed. And we found a bird feeder!
As he stopped in amazement, "But what of the creek?"
I remembered where we should play Hide-n-Go-Seek.

I forgot for a moment that he was a cat.
He was speaking my language so well. Fancy that!
And then a reminder jumped out of the bush.
He was hunting and prowling a bird to ambush!

"Oh no!" I exclaimed, as I chased and I cried
to keep that poor bird from having had died!
And then round the corner a hush fell so near
All was quiet and calm and there stood a deer.

The bird had escaped to its nest up above
and in place of the bird sat a beautiful dove.
The deer and the dove told me Phil had moved on
to the creek down the path that led into a pond.

In amazement and wonderment I never knew
that a deer and a dove could speak my language too!
So I took their advice and continued my path
to find Phil and a duck. They were having a bath!

"Oh my goodness!" I shouted, "Phil, I never knew
that you enjoyed ducks and a good cool swim too!"
Phil jumped out of the water and onto a rock
He told me a story. Yes, he really could talk!

He said all along he's been listening to me
But he just didn't know how he might make me see
that Hide-n-Go-Seek can be such a fun game,
where a cat and a human can speak language the same!

Randy
The Bossy Rooster

"I am rooster with so much to say
I begin by calling at the start of each day.
The sun rises quickly. I usually do too,
race the sun to its rising, calling cock-a-doodle-doo!"

"They say I am bossy but I don't think so
I'm just doing my job like a rooster should crow.
I can be a bit feisty and some think I am mean
I'm just doing a job here, taking care of my team."

"I dig and I hunt for bugs all day long
And when I hit jackpot I sing happy song!
My sweet good friend, Molly and her sister, Pink
They feed me and love me so full, I can't think!"

"And when I go home at the end of each day,
Pink and Molly have made me a nice coop to stay."
"Folks sometimes don't like me 'cause I make lots of noise,
But I voice my opinion because it's my choice."

"For I am a rooster so pretty and proud
With colors and feathers I must speak out loud!
I beg you don't harm me as so many do
when they don't like a rooster who sings cock-a-doodle-doo!"

"By morning and evening I'm just doing my job
To wake up the world and say night to Dad Bob."

"So if you don't like me, for a moment, I pray.
Just give me a chance till the end of the day."

"My job is not easy and I never knew
that being a rooster would be challenging too.
After learning about me, now you know what I do
There is certainly room for a rooster here too!"

"I'm busy and bossy but I care oh so much
about family, their safety and loving and such.
So if you were a rooster you might understand
that I'm proud and I want just a chance on this land."

"And when I awake you next morning so early
Remember I love you so sweet and so dearly.
And if I annoy you just give me a chance
In a moment you'll notice I think I can dance!"

The words of a rooster are precious and true
In the morning and evening he sings, "Cock-a-doodle-doo!"

Water Babies
Dawn and Dixie

Water babies Dawn and Dixie
have a frog friend that they call Pixie.
Dawn and Dixie love to splash
all day in water - they play and dash.

When Pixie joins them it's more fun.
There's three that splash now beneath the sun.

A frog named Pixie and ducks Dixie and Dawn
To them they're no different all wet in a pond.
They don't seem to mind much when it starts raining
In fact, they invite it and it's quite entertaining!

When Pixie goes home all worn out and soggy
The ducks they keep splashing though they miss their friend froggy.

These ducks they don't quack like other ducks do
But speak language softly, whispering, "Oh we thank you,
for loving us Molly and Pink as you do,
for filling our water and feeding us too."

"We may only be ducks at the end of the day
But we're ducks who communicate. We have something to say.
We are happy and grateful for our little lives
and tomorrow we'll show off our wonderful dives!"

"Into water and fountains again the fun starts
With Molly and Pink at the centre of our hearts!
Then Pixie will join us to start a new day
She's a green frog we know it. She just wants to play!"

"At the start of a duck's day we may lay an egg
For Molly to find it and keep it we beg.
For our eggs are your treasures, our special gifts too
to humans and families as special as you!"

"So eat them with pleasure and lots of care too
They were made from the love that we got from you!"

Suzy the Cat
Thinks She's a Princess!

Molly and Pink and their brother Jay

sat down to listen to Suzy one day.

It was amazing what she had to say.

She was humming and chirping and singing all day.

Black and white Suzy who looks like a cat,
She thinks she's a princess. Now imagine that!
But Suzy *is* special. She laughs and cries too.
She feels emotions just like me and you!

When Jay wouldn't listen to Suzy one day,
he pulled on her tail, "MEOW! That's not a good way
to treat a dear princess who has feelings too.
You hurt me so much Jay. Now I'm crying and blue."

For Suzy and others can feel the pain
So respect them, be gentle. Treat all life the same.

When Suzy stopped talking to Jay now you see
She feared him without trust and ran up a tree!
She shouted to others, "I won't come down till
Jay tells me he's sorry. Then maybe I will."

So Jay began listening to Suzy that day.
He said, "I'm so sorry. Come down please and play."
"Oh black and white Suzy high up in that tree,
I surely will show you how kind I can be."

"I won't pull your tail or cause you more pain
Now I know you can feel sad like me in the rain."
So Suzy came down and exclaimed, "I'm a princess!
I'm precious and special like you, I confess."

When Jay went to greet her now she did not run
and Jay began petting her under the sun.
As Suzy got closer to Jay that same day,
their friendship grew stronger as they started to play.

They were Princess and King of all Royalty
and Jay won her over of her loyalty!

"My name is Suzy. A princess as always
I'm special and feeling so happy most days.
Be gentle and loving and respectful too
cause I'm living and feeling exactly like you!"

Heart Talk, Hen Talk

There's something called "heart talk". Just sit still and listen.
If you're always talking, then there's something you're missin'.
Be still and be quiet and you surely will hear
the magic of language of all creatures dear.

Just start with the chickens. They've something to say.
Bach Bach Bach and What What for most of the day.
But what does Bach Bach Bach and What What What mean?
You'll have to sit longer to hear where they've been.

Dear Emma and Miley and their babies too,
follow Randy the rooster as they know they should do.
For Randy protects them from danger – Big Birds
that want to swoop down and swallow their words!

Bach Bach Bach and What What are they really saying?
"It's our way, a hen's way of hoping and praying.
That you will be kind to our feathers and more
while we live in your family, walk through the same door."

"Your house we don't live in. We sleep in a coop.
We don't eat the same things as you – chicken soup!
But if ever you must take our dear lives one day
Please do it in kindness together we pray."

"We give you our eggs that are lovingly laid
So if you must eat us recall what we made.
For people eat chickens, but please hear our chatter
For food you must use us it just does not matter."

"We are brave and courageous and all we can say,
Bach Bach Bach and What What and silently pray,
That there won't be suffering and no fear or pain,
when our lives you must take all in love - in God's name."

"We feel and we worry and pray just like you
that you'll thank us, respect us, and live so well too.
'Cause now we are in you - our souls living too,
Saying Bach Bach and What What - How much we love you!"

For being so gentle when we had to go,
For living with kindness and treating us so.
Be still and just listen to what we are saying
It's heart talk, it's hen talk. It's all we are praying."

Alfie and Ruby
Best of Friends

Alfie the horse and Ruby the goat,
They don't look alike, but they both wear a coat.
"I dress in brown", says Ruby, "you know."
And Alf wears a nice coat as white as the snow.

Ruby treats Alfie like he's her big brother.
You simply will not find one without the other.
Although these two best friends look nothing alike,
They follow each other each day on a hike.

And one thing's for certain, with Alf you'll see Ruby
Singing a song they call Scooby Doob Dooby!
When Alf tries to dress not in white but in brown
As he rolls in the dirt, Ruby has a big frown.

She says, "You are not brown my dear best friend, Alf
You're more like the milk that comes out of myself!"
When our mother, Wendy, she milks me below,
that wonderful liquid – yes it's milk white as snow!"

"And you are a beautiful pure white horse too
So don't try to change, Alf, because I love you
the way that you are - a talking white horse
who guides me and loves me - my best friend, of course!"

"Oh Ruby, you must know I surely do love you.
Your brown coat is awesome and I want one too!
Because I get bored with my white coat sometimes."
"But white is so pretty", Ruby pipes in and chimes.

"You're beautiful always, both inside and out.
I really don't get what you're talking about
when you try so hard to look just like me.
You're a horse, not a goat dear. It's plain, can't you see?"

"You're thoughtful and lovely in every way.
Be you Alf, be true Alf, I tell you, I say."

"Oh thank you, dear Ruby for helping me see,
I'm not you, my best friend. I simply am ME!
One thing that is certain for sure I *do* know.
Our hearts look the same now all warm in a glow."

For best friends they will be. It just does not matter
that one might be smaller or one might be fatter!
Their hearts now are beating with love and compassion
for them and their family in a warm caring fashion.

"So don't try to change, Alf, your white coat to brown
I love you in white Alf! Let's go and lie down."
And Ruby laughs loudly when Alf lies down too
He gets up all dirty. "I'm brown now like you!"

"Ha ha!", Alf laughs louder and lets out a nay.
"Now let's go have more fun and roll in the hay!
You're so fun to be with and play jokes on too.
I look just like you now! Ha ha! Jokes on you!"

And Ruby and Alf now, they just have their way
of making us all laugh at some point each day!
For best friends are awesome and wonderful too.
We all need a best friend – and someone like YOU!

So hear Alf and Ruby take turns one another.
Their laughter and humor and love for each other.
Alf the big white horse and brown Ruby too.
Together they spell LOVE - in all hearts – in YOU!

Forest City
"Here We Come!"

One evening quite late the moon shining full,
The McPhersons decided their life was too dull.
"We need an adventure", said Pink, Jay and Molly.
Then Wendy exclaimed, "By gosh, oh by golly!"

"What kind of adventure do you think you're all seeking?"
Bob made it a game, told them, "There is no peeking!"
"Let's put all our names in a bucket to share
and take turns each picking to see what we dare."

"For what is adventure but plenty of fun?
We have to be willing and able to run!"

"But what do you mean, Dad? But what should we do?"
"Think up an adventure that *we* can do too.
So write down your name and your idea too
'bout what an adventure just might be to you."

So all of the people in this family
came up with a plan, an adventure to be.

It had to include all the animals too
like Randy and Philly and Emma and Sue.
And Alfie and Ruby and Dixie and Dawn
and Miley with baby who we have named Fawn.

Think up and adventure that you'd like to do.
Tomorrow we'll draw names and plan it out too.

The sun hit the window in the morning dew
when Randy awoke first singing "cock-a-doodle-doo!"

Then Emma and Miley and Baby Fawn too
sprang out from their chick coop to greet the day new.

Cats Philly and Suzy were next to arise,
slowly stretching and yawning, wiping sleep from their eyes.
Phil jumped onto Molly and Sue onto Jay.
Then Pink began waking to start a new day.

And dear Dawn and Dixie making sounds like the loons
started humming and singing their favorite tunes.
They were all so excited to be part of the fun
in today's family outing beneath the warm sun.

Now all that is missing are Ruby and Alf.
They say they'll be waiting with their 'deer' friend, Ralph.

Into the forest and out to the trees.
An adventure got pulled from the bucket, Dad sees!
But how will they do it - fifteen of them go?
Just line up, get ready and before it you'll know!

So into the forest and out to the trees.
They all started marching with feet, legs and knees.
So to Forest City, "Oh here we come!"
The McPhersons are off for a day of great fun!

Dad heads up the line-up, then Mom and Pink too,
then all of the animals - Gosh, it looks like a zoo!
And Molly and Jay at the end of the pack
have the sun and the wind and the bees at their back.

They get to the forest delighted to meet
dear Ruby and Alfie bent down at their feet!
"Welcome McPhersons to this Forest City
We often hang out here gettin dirty and gritty."

There's always adventure in this little town.
Keep marching, keep walking, keep coming on down.

The path is a winding to the 'Sit Tea Haul'.
Sit down and enjoy here some tea with a doll.
Then follow the sign that says 'Horse Apple Way'.
It will lead you through 'Bored Walk' and a meadow of play!

Now play in the meadow as long as you like,
before we move on and continue our hike.
Into the forest and out to the trees,
a great fun adventure with even the bees!

"Oh no!" exclaimed Molly, "But there is a bear!"
They all started screaming. It gave them a scare!
But big white horse, Alfie, stepped in in a hurry,
Said, "I will protect you. Don't run, do not worry."

For bears don't like horses 'cause horses are bigger,
than bears for the most part like this one named 'Tigger'.
"I don't want to harm you although you may think"
Then the bear disappeared just as quick as a wink.

The McPhersons were frozen, bewildered and frightened,
But Alf and dear Ruby whose senses were heightened,
Said "Follow us down to the bridge that we know
to the safety and comfort of a pretty rainbow!"

"But it isn't raining!" said Wendy and Bob.
"I'm thirsty, I'm hungry", Pink started to sob.
So follow the path to the water, you'll see
you can drink there and rest there on 'Pirate Property'.

Here no one will harm you and you can just rest.
Relax here, have fun here till you feel your best.
But Miley said, "Ruby, I can't get across
with Fawn here too little, she'll get lost in the moss!"

Jay had an idea as he shouted to Fawn,
"Get on Miley's back, Chick, with Dixie and Dawn!"
"The four of you can cross that bridge all together
It's effort and teamwork in all kinds of weather."

So Miley, her baby, and Dixie and Dawn
They did it! They made it! With tiny babe Fawn!

Now Philly and Suzy lost in "Sit Tea Haul",
Alf, Ruby - they noticed and started to call.
"Here kitties, here kitties, Come down to the creek.
Dear Philly and Suzy, it's you two we seek!"

When Phil came out bounding with Suzy behind him
"We're glad that you noticed and called on a whim."
"We heard you and chortled, but couldn't get out
And when no one could hear us we fussed all about!"

"Keep calling, keep calling, oh please everyone!
We want to come join you and play in the sun!"
And Suzy broke free from the town hall just when
the calling was loudest just exactly then!

And Phil took the lead as they scurried together,
through forest and trees, through all kinds of weather!
Until they arrived at the sunshine where all
were laughing and playing and having a ball!

Into the forest and out through the trees.
The adventure is over, the family all sees.

When darkness has fallen and night has come too
Not one family member is sad or is blue.
'Cause they have each other, much more and then some.
This adventure is over and the next one to come.

So into the forest and out through the trees.
Next time the adventure will begin with the bees!

Watch for BOOK TWO when
"Molly meets Bees, Birds, Bugs and Butterflies!"

About the Author

Tracey L Kehler

As a lover of all life, Tracey holds that her truest friends and teachers are the animals she seeks to help. A believer in freedom and living well, Tracey spreads this philosophy to all who share their lives with her for any length of time. "A good life is not necessarily a long life", she states, "as freedom poses risks in all the goodness of living well. Life is about quality, not quantity. I always feel blessed, like the lucky one, when I have the opportunity to learn about a new life and enhance it by sheltering it, feeding it and loving that life to the best of my ability. That is my divine purpose. I am the lucky one to have the company of every soulful creature that crosses onto my path."

Tracey's belief that "everyone has a book to write" doesn't stop at people. Her compassion for animals tells countless stories of their struggles, hardships, life journeys, rewards, disappointments and challenges. "Animals are just like us. Perhaps the only difference is their language." Tracey has spent countless hours advocating for animal welfare and volunteering for animal charities.

The passion that Tracey holds in her heart for other species has led her onto a path of animal communication and energy healing. Having come from a number of years of working in the healing arts for people with body work, massage and healing touch, Tracey's journey has led her to working more specifically with the animal kingdom. Through her own experiences with past life regression, shamanism and animal totem studies, Tracey continues to strive to understand animals, why they are in our lives, and the messages they bring to us on a deeper level. Her aim is to help other people realize that we can all hear the animals...if only we stop to listen. Most often, if we hear them, we can correct problematic behaviors and conditions to create more overall harmony in the home.

Having obtained a BSW degree (social work), Tracey has taken her passion to help make a difference beyond people. She holds values of compassion and respect for all life and believes that if we can tap into these core values and teach people at an early age to communicate and listen to other life forms, perhaps we can see a chance for a more peaceful world where all species can coexist on this earth peacefully together in harmony.

Tracey lives on beautiful Vancouver Island, BC, Canada with her partner in life, a host of farm animals, and her two special cats who traveled back to Canada with her all the way from Costa Rica.

About the Illustrator

Kara LaRose

Kara is a talented and gifted young artist who cares passionately about children and their holistic development. Her work encompasses everything from providing care and guidance to children with developmental and behavioural disabilities, to drawing, painting, sculpting, and photography. She recognizes the value of creativity and play in all aspects of life, enjoying singing, dancing and connecting with nature.

Kara's clairsentience and native spirit are gifts that she has mentored and brings to all she does. Her love of nature and animals is evident in her work as an artist. She is an extra special gift to the making of this children's collection.

Kara presently lives in Red Deer, Alberta where she was born and raised, close to those near and dear to her heart – her cherished family. She works full time guiding, supporting and teaching young children of Aboriginal ancestry, sharing knowledge of the culture and learning through play.

Printed in the United States
By Bookmasters